Michael Ipgrave

CHRIST IN TEN THOUSAND PLACES

A Catholic Perspective on
Christian Encounter with other Faiths

DARTON · LONGMAN + TODD

Published by Darton, Longman and Todd, 1 Spencer Court, 140–142 Wandsworth High Street, London SW18 4JJ in association with Affirming Catholicism, St Mary-le-Bow, Cheapside, London EC2V 6AU.

ISBN 0–232–52079–8

The views expressed in this booklet are those of the author and do not necessarily reflect any policy of Affirming Catholicism.

Booklets designed by Bet Ayer, phototypeset by Intype, London and printed by Halstan and Co Ltd, Amersham, Bucks.

CONTENTS

'Christ plays in ten thousand places,
Lovely in limbs, and lovely in eyes not his
To the Father through the features of men's faces'
[Gerard Manley Hopkins, *'As Kingfishers Catch Fire'*]

Affirming Catholicism

Affirming Catholicism has never been, and is not intended to be, yet another 'party' within the Church of England or the Anglican Communion but rather a movement of encouragement and hope.

A group of lay people and clergy met together in 1990 to identify that authentic Catholic tradition within the Church which appeared to be under threat. Wider support was expressed at a public meeting on 9 June 1990 in London and at a residential conference in York in July 1991.

Since then Affirming Catholicism has been afforded charitable status. The following statement is extracted from the Trust Deed:

> It is the conviction of many that a respect for scholarship and free enquiry has been characteristic of the Church of England and of the Churches of the wider Anglican Communion from earliest times and is fully consistent with the status of those Churches as part of the Holy Catholic Church. It is desired to establish a charitable educational foundation which will be true both to those characteristics and to the Catholic tradition within Anglicanism . . . The object of the foundation shall be the advancement of education in the doctrines and the historical development of the Church of England and the Churches of the wider Anglican Communion, as held by those professing to stand within the Catholic tradition.

In furtherance of these aims and objectives, Affirming Catholicism is producing this series of booklets. The series will encompass two sets of books: one set will attempt to present a clear, well-argued Catholic viewpoint on issues of debate facing the Church at any given time; the other set will cover traditional doctrinal themes. The editor of the series is Jeffrey John; the first four titles in the series were: *Imagining Jesus – An Introduction to the Incarnation* by Lewis Ayres; *Why Women Priests? – The Ordination of Women and the Apostolic Ministry* by Jonathan Sedgwick; *History, Tradition and Change – Church History and the Development of Doctrine* by Peter Hinchliff; *'Permanent, Faithful, Stable' – Christian Same-sex Partnerships* by Jeffrey John. Other titles are: *Politics and the Faith Today – Catholic Social Vision for the 1990s* by Kenneth Leech; *'Is the Anglican Church Catholic?' – The Catholicity of Anglicanism* by Vincent Strudwick; *'Making Present' – The Practice of Catholic Life and Liturgy* by Christopher Irvine.

To order these publications individually or on subscription, or for enquiries regarding the aims and activities of Affirming Catholicism write to:

The Secretary
Mainstream
St Mary-le-Bow
Cheapside
London EC2V 6AU

Tel: 071–329 4070

Introduction

'We believe in, and confess, one God, admittedly in a different way'[1]: those words of a Christian to a Muslim could have come from a contemporary 'pluralist' theologian. In fact, they are taken from a letter written more than nine hundred years ago, by a man of unimpeachable orthodoxy, Pope Gregory VII. I mention them because they point to two features of inter-faith encounter which are sometimes forgotten today.

First, inter-faith issues may be facing British Christians with a new intensity today, but they have been on the church's agenda since the beginning. The apostolic and patristic church established its identity within a religiously diverse environment; the evangelisation of Europe was a gradual process in which encounter with non-Christian patterns of worship played a shaping role; Christians in Asia and Africa have lived for centuries in multi-faith societies.

Secondly, throughout the centuries Christians have sought to respond to these issues in a variety of ways. The self-proclaimed 'traditionalism' or 'orthodoxy' of a narrow exclusivism in fact represents only one strand among several, and that not necessarily the most persuasive. I would claim that the mainstream of catholic Christianity suggests a much more open and affirmative attitude towards people of other faiths; in the following pages I seek to justify this claim.

This is not to say, however, that we can simply investigate the tradition we have inherited and find there guidelines for correct attitudes to inter-faith questions. Rather, we must begin from the lived reality of Christian encounter with people of faith in Britain today and look at the issues this encounter throws up; we bring to this encounter the resources of Christian tradition, as those we meet also bring the riches of their own living traditions.

So I will begin with the situation which I know best as a place of inter-faith encounter, the city of Leicester, and set down a few simple stories of everyday meetings with people of living faith. The following six sections touch briefly on a range of issues which emerge from such meetings: pastoral care, community relations, environmental awareness, evangelism, Christology, and spirituality and worship.

Living in Leicester

'With the drawing of this Love and the voice of this Calling
We shall not cease from exploration'

T. S. Eliot, '*Little Gidding*'

'None of us is nowhere, all of us are somewhere', it has been said, and we must begin in the place where we are, the immediate context within which we live out and think out our faith.

I am in Leicester. So let me begin by mentioning a few things about living in Leicester. Leicester has a population of about 300,000, making it a medium-sized city in British terms. Big enough to host a rich and varied civic life, it is still small enough to have a real sense of corporate identity. In 1990, that corporate identity found expression in Leicester's designation as Britain's first 'Environment City'; the surrounding county has been chosen as the site for a new National Forest. Like other cities, Leicester has its urban priority areas, particularly in the inner zone; the regeneration of social and economic life in these neighbourhoods has been a priority shared by local and national authorities, commerce and the voluntary sector, including organised communities of faith.

Of those communities, members of religions other than Christianity constitute probably between a quarter and a third of the city's population. Figures can only be estimates, but at around 50,000 the largest group are Hindus (mostly of Gujarati-speaking Indian descent): after Durban, Leicester has the biggest Hindu community in the world outside India. There are around 20,000 Muslims and 15,000 Sikhs in the city, and smaller but significant communities of Jains, Jews, Buddhists and Bahais. Most of these faith groups have their own places of worship, and the coming and going of people on their way to and from prayer is a marked feature of many parts of the inner city. Alongside the temples, mosques, and gurdwaras there are countless Asian shops, businesses, and social centres; and at the great festivals like Diwali, Eid, and Vaisakhi (not forgetting Christmas), the streets are bright with illuminations and decorations.

Leicester also, of course, has a complete range of Christian churches, including many organised and led by members of the Afro-Caribbean community and a few comprising predominantly Asian Christians. Ecumenical co-operation between most of these churches is an established fact of life, and many are deeply involved in the life of their local neighbourhoods.

I work within this diverse religious scene as an Anglican priest with special responsibility for building up links between Christians and other faith communities. This has led me into close and deep friendships with many people of faiths and cultures far different from my own, and I have found that a profoundly enriching experience. It has also been my good fortune to be based for part of my time at Leicester's Jain Centre. At present Britain's only consecrated temple of this ancient faith, the Centre is a magnificent adaptation of traditional Indian sacred architecture housed in the buildings of a converted Congregational church.

The reflections which follow originate in what might be described as a dialogue between two factors. One is this context of multi-faith Leicester, the other is the Christian faith I have inherited through the Catholic tradition; I believe that tradition to have a universal quality which provides analysis and vision apposite to any situation or context. The meeting of those two factors, the universal and the particular, is not free of tension; in my experience it is essentially a creative tension, pointing to patterns through which I can affirm the living faith of the church in ways which honour and engage with the no-less-living faith of friends and neighbours outside the church. Other Christians will perhaps be pointed to other patterns, for there is great diversity both in the encounters we make with people of other faiths and in the traditions within which we reflect on those encounters, but I believe that we will all often be able to echo the words of Michael Barnes:

> When faith meets faith, truth does not confront falsity, rather we are speaking of communities of men and women struggling to come to terms with ultimate reality. Christians share that struggle. Theology in a pluralist world begins and ends with the conversation, with learning over and over again the meaning and the implications of the act of faith.[2]

Meeting in Faith

'In friendship eternity blossoms, truth shines forth, and charity grows sweet; consider whether you ought to separate the name of wisdom from these three'

St Aelred of Rievaulx, *'De Spiritali Amicitia'*

Encounters

I am sitting on the floor in a gurdwara [Sikh temple] in Leicester enjoying a tasty Punjabi meal. The Sikh sitting next to me is talking to me about the grief he felt on the death of his wife from cancer two months previously. But he explains to me that he knows he and his wife have been truly united as souls, and not even death can sever that. He loves to come every evening to the gurdwara to worship, for in the presence of the holy scripture and singing the praises of God he experiences a deep sense of union with his wife. As I listen, I recall my loss when my mother died five years ago, and the way in which I sometimes feel particularly close to her when I celebrate the eucharist, and I tell him so. We both go home that night with a new sense of wonder at the depths of the spirit who helps us to bear one another's burdens.

In the hall of a Methodist church, I am introducing an ecumenical group of theological students to a speaker who will present them with a view of 'The Islamic Community in Britain'. Many of them have quite definite preconceptions about the Islamic community, but the speaker completely surprises them. He openly admits that Muslims in Britain face problems of division, secularisation, identity, and so on, but he goes on to point out the tremendous and explosive resource his community has in the Qur'an – 'spiritual dynamite', he calls it. If Muslims were really to open themselves to the challenge of this book, he says, they would be a dynamic force in building up the life of Britain. 'How nice to hear a Muslim who is moderate', one of the students says to me afterwards; I reply that rarely have I heard a message so challengingly radical from anybody of any faith.

Into the office of the Jain Centre walks a young Jain social worker. She has come to photocopy a petition asking for more green open spaces for children to play in a deprived inner area of the city. She tells me that as a Jain she thinks it vital that children should learn to live with and respect the natural world. I agree, but I feel I have learnt this lesson as I was brought up in a country village. As we talk I am distracted by a fly buzzing around; I try to swat it, and miss. 'Good,' she says laughing, 'that is one bit of needless harm to a living being that has been avoided'. I feel a mixture of amusement, irritation and shame, and wonder if perhaps I need to think further about my respect for the natural world after all, and I remember William Blake's poem:

Little fly, thy summer's play
My thoughtless hand has brush'd away.

Am not I a fly like thee?
Or art not thou a man like me?[3]

It is early December, and dusk is gathering in the park. I stand in a crowd of Jews and Gentiles around a gigantic eight-branched metal candlestick erected by a busy roundabout. The rabbi explains the significance of the eight-day festival of Hanukkah. Remembering the defeat of the Syrian oppressors by the Maccabean heroes and their cleansing and rededication of the temple, the Jews will each day light one branch of the candle in celebration of the freedom and hope which the Lord gives to his people. When the sun is down, the light is switched on, and the children of the Hebrew community sing their well-practised songs, then erupt into a lively dance, joined by many of the adults, before we all share in delicious Jewish sweetmeats. As we leave the park, the candle's light shines on in the darkness, witness to the good news of the God of Israel who saves and sets free.

I have taken my friend Jinaratana, a Buddhist monk from Sri Lanka living in a small vihara (Buddhist monastery) in suburban Leicester, to the nearby Roman Catholic monastery of Mount St Bernard, in the wide open spaces of Charnwood Forest. We climb the impressive Calvary, crowned by the cross of Jesus, then descend the steep path on the other side to the chapel of the pieta, where a lifelike figure of the crucified Lord lies supported by his sorrowful mother. Jinaratana ponders this for some time, and then explains that he is remembering the rock-carved figures in Sri Lanka showing the Buddha lying down, passing into nirvana at his departure from the world. Although that is a more peaceful scene, Jinaratana says, both Jesus and Buddha have a look of compassion on their faces; he thinks that Jesus must have been a truly enlightened being to radiate such compassion. I am deeply aware of the closeness we feel in gazing together on the face of the crucified Jesus; aware too of the way that faith in Jesus as risen and living makes a profound difference to the way that I understand him.

The May Festival of Our Lady of Walsingham is always a colourful occasion in the Leicester church year. Starting from St Andrew's Church, we carry a statue of Mary around the streets of the deprived inner-city parish, returning to the church for a sumptuous mass. This year, I have invited my friend Ramesh, a devout Hindu, to join us. The sky is dark and threatening, but he comes without any kind of waterproof clothing. When I express surprise, he shames me by replying 'Do you not have faith?' But when a few drops begin to fall he assures me: 'The rain is a sign of divine grace and blessing on your procession.'

As we walk along the streets, people open their doors or look through their windows to see what the noise is all about. Some appear curious, some amused, a few irritated; one man enjoys the opportunity of turning up his sound system as loud as he can in an attempt to drown our singing. But Ramesh is deeply impressed by these people showing an interest in what is happening, and has no doubt about the significance of their curiosity: 'It is good', he says, 'that so many people wish to have a **darshana** (having sight in a context of worship) of the Divine Mother, and to receive her blessings.'

Back in church for the mass, Ramesh finds particular pleasure in singing one of the hymns, which expresses the worshipper's devotion to the mother of Jesus:

> As I kneel before you,
> as I bow my head in prayer,
> take this day, make it yours
> and fill me with your love.
>
> As I kneel before you,
> And I see your smiling face,
> every thought, every word
> is lost in your embrace.

Ramesh tells me that he had felt tears welling up in his eyes as he sang this, for it was a perfect expression of the Hindu ideal of **bhakti** (service of the deity through loving devotion); he is more firmly convinced now than ever that Hindus and Christians are walking on the same journey of pilgrimage to the one God whom nobody has ever seen.

Meanings

As those examples show, meetings with people of other faiths can take place in many different contexts and raise many different issues for Christians. Many of these issues have caused considerable controversy within the churches in recent years, and probably will continue to do so. Yet we must always remember that they have their origin, not as theoretical problems within the life of the church, but as real situations. In my experience of such meetings the integrity of my faith is hardly ever threatened, nor is the living reality of my neighbour's faith belittled. On the contrary, a genuinely affirmative approach means that it is possible to be surely and confidently oneself as a Christian and at the same time to rejoice in the faith of the other – and it is important to remember that this is true both of those areas where we find common ground and of those in which we agree to differ.

If we forget the rootedness of inter-faith issues in personal encounter, then our discussion of those issues becomes arid and divorced from the reality of our situation. What is worse, we lose out on the enriching friendships with our non-Christian brothers and sisters which can so deepen our own faith, enlighten our own understanding, and renew our own discipleship.

Supporting One Another

'At the evening of life, you will be examined in love'

St John of the Cross, '*Sayings of Light and Love*'

People of other faiths are first and foremost people; they experience joys and suffer sorrows as we do. This is an obvious point, yet it is forgotten whenever people rely on stereotyped images which they picked up from closed mono-cultural circles at home, at work, or in their community. It was against just such a background of a depersonalised stereotype of Jewish people that Shakespeare put into the mouth of his Jewish merchant of Venice words stressing the humanity he shared with Christians:

> Is not a Jew fed with the same food, hurt with the same weapons, subject to the same diseases, healed by the same means, warmed and cooled by the same winter and summer as a Christian is? – if you prick us do we not bleed? if you tickle us do we not laugh?[4]

But, like the Jews of Shylock's Venice, many people of other faiths living in Britain today face some particular problems. Almost all Muslims, Hindus and Sikhs are of a different ethnic group to the majority of the UK population, and in large measure they participate in a different culture. The older members of the communities were born outside Britain, most of them either in the Indian subcontinent or in East Africa: the majority of children and younger people were born here, but are significantly formed by the language, customs, and cultures of their homes.

As a result, people of non-Christian faith frequently encounter the racism endemic in many areas of British society. Sometimes this means direct personal abuse or ridicule, but more frequent is what has been termed 'institutional racism', the failure – mostly quite unintended – of organised society to enable them to participate fully in its structures and to respond to their needs in areas such as housing, employment, health care, education, and political representation. They may find themselves in situations where they do not have access to basic requirements such as a place for the offering of prayer for Muslims or pure vegetarian food for Hindus. They may find themselves unable to communicate their needs because of an absence of translation facilities. They may find what are for them basic personal norms of courtesy, modesty, or hospitality being violated by others who are not attuned to their culture. They may experience their faith being misunderstood, caricatured, or ignored in situations where they believe it should be noticed and honoured. Christians of all races will also often experience this slighting of their faith, and black Christians will also encounter racism, sometimes even within the churches. Most white people in Britain today, though, are not likely to have firsthand experiences of the wide range of problems met by people of other faiths.

Such problems can be especially grievous when they come at times of personal suffering – sickness, unemployment, family stress, bereavement. Hospitalisation, for example, is a traumatic experience for anybody, of any faith or none, but people of non-Christian faith and culture may feel themselves to be in an acutely alien environment, cut off from the normal support of family and community, and generally experiencing disorientation and confusion. Health authorities have made tremendous efforts over the past few years to address the needs of patients of every faith and culture, but it is perhaps inevitable that people in situations of physical disorder should feel their spiritual integrity called into question also.

What guidance does the Catholic tradition give to Christians involved in any way in such situations of personal suffering? We may surely look here to the pattern of the incarnation as archetypal: in Jesus we see the story of God encountering at first hand the sufferings of humanity, being a channel of healing grace within those sufferings, yet also himself being supported in his own suffering by the help of others. These three dimensions of the divine involvement in Christ point us to three ways in which Christians too may be incarnationally involved.

First, Christians will often find themselves in positions of pastoral care of people of other faiths – for example, as doctors, nurses, or other medical staff; as ordained ministers; as volunteers; as friends or neighbours. Pastoral involvement here begins from the incarnational principle of meeting people where they are and as they are. In multi-faith situations, that means that differences in religion or culture, theological or ethical judgments, and preconceived opinions about other faiths should never be allowed to stand in the way of genuine encounter at the deepest level. We will be aware of people of another faith first of all as fellow human beings, and we will look for ways in which we can support them. As with all pastoral ministry, this will involve listening carefully to people's understandings of their own situation, their needs, hopes, and fears; in the case of a committed member of another faith, it will involve particularly careful attention to the framework of meaning and values by which their experience is being interpreted. Very often, this may differ in important ways from the approach that the Christian would naturally bring to the same experience; it is important that we should be both aware of this and comfortable with it – a pastoral crisis may not, for example, be the most appropriate time at which to engage in discussion on the validity or otherwise of a philosophy of karmic reward and punishment.

Understanding human fulfilment as involving bodily and spiritual health, right relationships with family and friends, a recognised and useful role in society, and an overall vision of the meaning and purpose of human life within the gracious purposes of God, Christians will want to support people of other faiths in their quest for meaning and purpose in their lives. In pastoral situations, this will often mean putting them in touch with appropriate sources of help and advice in the wider community to whom they would not otherwise have obvious access. In certain cases – particularly in ministry in institutions such as hospitals or prisons – it may in fact mean helping them to establish contact with the appropriate person in their own faith community; other religious groups do not in general have the organised chaplaincy services operated by mainline churches.

Secondly, we take the incarnational approach one stage further when we realise that often Christians in their own loving presence can embody the grace and compassion of God to their neighbours. This can be particularly evident in the case of ordained ministers, who are widely understood by those outside their own tradition of faith to be in some sense representatives of God, or at least 'holy persons' in some more undefined way. For example, it is not unknown for a Christian priest to be asked to offer prayers in a Hindu home after a bereavement. At the lowest level, this may mean that he is being asked to act as a ritual specialist because nobody else appropriate is available; on the other hand, it can show that a genuine ministry of unquestioning compassion and spiritual power is being recognised and accepted. Whatever response he makes, the priest will want to ensure that he acts with integrity and with respect for the integrity of those who ask him; but he will also want to affirm that which is of God in the faith that led to the request.

Finally, we must remember that Christians will not always be the 'givers' and others the 'receivers'. 'It is more blessed to give than to receive,' St Paul recorded Jesus as having said (Acts 20.35); he may well have been right, yet for many it is certainly more difficult to receive than to give. In a society like our own which is geared to achievement, it can be very hard even for faithful Christians to accept that they too are in need of support, help, and compassion. But there are times in our lives when we will find ourselves 'on the receiving end' through misfortune, sickness, bereavement, or whatever, and it may well be that those who are ministering to us in such situations are in fact people of other faiths – whether professionals, friends, or neighbours.

In such circumstances, we may penetrate to a yet deeper understanding of what an incarnational approach to life is about as we learn that receiving too has a blessedness about it. To be weak, vulnerable, dependent on and open to others' kindness, as was the incarnate Son of God, is to be in the same position as the man by the roadside helped by the Good Samaritan, who would have been to him a person of another faith (Luke 10.29ff). We should also remember here the 'hungry, thirsty, naked, sick, imprisoned' people for visiting whom the righteous sheep on the right hand of the King received eternal joy (Matthew 25.31ff). To grasp the full import of Matthew's parable, we need to appreciate that these 'little ones' were in fact for him members of the Christian community, while the sheep, as members of 'the nations', are in modern terms 'people of other faiths'. It was through their support of their brothers and sisters that the powerful compassion of God was ministered; in experiencing a like compassion today through the kindness of their neighbours of other faiths many ordinary Christians are likewise coming to know blessing – like 'Granny', for example.

> She was an elderly white woman. The majority of her neighbours were Gujarati-speaking Hindus. She found their food and clothes and language not offensive, but strange and rather forbidding. So she kept herself to herself, not wanting to be rude, but uncertain how to make friends.
>
> Her husband had cancer. He became terminally ill, and went into hospital. She was alone in the house, and there was a knock on the door. It was a small boy from next door. 'My dad would like to take you to see your husband', he said. So, grateful for the offer of a lift in the dark, she accepted. The man from next door spoke little English, but every day until her husband died he took her to see him in hospital. The driver and his passenger learned to communicate through smiles and laughter, through photos of family members which they showed one another. When this sort of understanding failed, his youngsters, whose English was perfect, helped out; they used to pile into the car and go along for the ride.
>
> The woman's husband died, slowly and painfully. She was grief-stricken. Her neighbour brought her back from her final visit to hospital. A little while later came a knock at her door. It was the neighbour's little boy. They said nothing, but went into her front room. He slipped his hand into hers, and they sat there together in silence. Eventually, he went away, but came back with his mother. She spoke hardly any English, but put her arms around the other woman and they wept together. Then the neighbour went into the kitchen and heated up some food she had brought, and stayed until some of it, at least, had been eaten.
>
> Almost every day after that, there was contact between the white woman and her neighbours until she died. She was so pleased that the children of the family began to call her 'Granny'. Just before she died, she confided to her minister that getting to know her neighbours was one of the best things that had ever happened to her.[5]

Building Communities

'When planning action man's reason shares God's eternal law by nature, knowing some general principles but not the detailed plans which the eternal law lays down for each single thing'

St Thomas Aquinas, *Summa Theologiae 1a 91.3*

The biblical story is one of a God who forms people into communities – the children of Israel, the catholic church – with whom he enters into a relation of partnership. That is to say, through the incarnation of the Son and the inspiration of the Spirit, God meets people where they are and by gathering them together empowers them to become channels through whom his kingdom may come. Indeed, the stress on community lies at the centre of Catholic doctrine in the claim that it is a pattern not just for the Creator's relationship with the created order, but also for the inner life of the Creator himself: the doctrine of the Holy Trinity can be seen as a picture of three divine persons co-inhering in an endless and endlessly creative partnership, each responding fully to the other within a community.

Community is an important theme in many other faith traditions too. For example, in Islam the **ummah**, the worldwide brotherhood of the faithful, binds together Muslims through the law of God which both confers privileges on them and requires duties of them. Again, among Sikhs the **khalsa**, the 'order' of those who have visibly committed themselves to loyal service of the Guru, provides for its members a coherent and ordered communal way of life which finds visible expression in the **langar**, the common kitchen of a gurdwara where meals are freely served to all comers. Church, **ummah**, **khalsa**, and other expressions of religious community differ significantly in the ways they account for the obligations which bind them together, but they agree in understanding faith as a pattern of life to be lived within a community committed to and itself constituted by the same pattern.

This communal understanding, shared in different ways by people of every major faith tradition, must be set against a secularised understanding of religion which concedes space for faith only as an individual pursuit of 'the religious', those who like that sort of thing, who may be allowed or even encouraged to indulge their hobby so long as it does not interfere with anybody else. Many Christians have become so accustomed to viewing their faith in this privatised way that a renewed awareness of the communal dimension can be an unwelcome shock. However, there is no doubt that such an awareness is present and growing in the world today: globally and nationally, it is becoming increasingly apparent that religions are here to stay. They already play an important part in the political life of many nations internally and externally, but they surely possess an even greater potential than has been generally realised.

That potential, we must remember, is essentially ambivalent – it can cause division and destruction, or it can build up reconciliation and reconstruction. Indeed, awareness of the double-edged power of faith in political life is an explicit theme in the three great prophetic traditions which look back to Abraham, founder of a new community, as an exemplar of faith. So, for example, Jeremiah is set by the Lord 'over nations and over kingdoms, to pluck up and to break down, to destroy and to overthrow, to build and to plant' (Jeremiah 1:10). Jesus too is both the one who comes to bring 'not peace on earth, but division' (Luke 12.51f) and at the same time 'himself our peace, who has made us one, and broken down the dividing wall of hostility' (Ephesians 2.14). Again, the Qur'an lays stress both on the primal unity of humanity as willed by God and on the fearful reality of divisions based on religious differences (e.g. Surah 2.213).

Renewed awareness of the significance of religion is in Britain partly a result of the articulate and persuasive example of non-Christian faith groups, especially the Muslim community. Christians have cause to be grateful to their Muslim brothers and sisters for firmly putting faith back onto the political map of Britain in recent years. And Christians must consequently acknowledge also that: 'the faith that is back on the social and political map of Britain is definitely faith expressed in the variety and diversity of a multi-faith society'.[6]

In what kind of communities does faith find expression? For the 'privatised' account of religion, the only role for a faith community would seem to be that of an association of people who share a common interest, a kind of club for people who like meeting together. In reality, members of faith communities have widely differing interests and opinions, and their commitment to membership rests on something much more deep-seated than a predilection for certain kinds of activity or certain ways of thought. This diversity is readily apparent in traditions like Christianity, Islam or Buddhism, which have an international mission and membership; but it would be quite wrong to suppose that more ethnically defined faiths like Hinduism, Sikhism or Judaism are monolithic entities. Not only do all these communities include many different subgroups, but also within any given group there is a wide variety of patterns of individual belief and practice. Furthermore, the very experience of living out faith in a secularised post-industrial society has resulted in different individuals and families adopting different strategies of adaptation and survival.

In this context of rapid social change, many – both within and without faith communities – understandably wonder if they will in fact be able to survive; the continuing transmission of faith to the next generation is a major concern for Muslims, Hindus, Jews and others in Britain, as well as for Christians. But religions are remarkably resilient phenomena, because the cohesion of their diverse communities is supplied, not by shared interests, but by shared visions of ultimate reality. Those visions often find their most powerful expression in sacred stories around which the communiy unite, stories which are celebrated in festivals that provide a rhythm to the community's life – the story of Ram and Sita at Diwala, the story of Guru Gobind Singh at Vaisakhi, of Esther and Haman at Purim, of Jesus, Mary and Joseph at Christmas, and so on. These stories of faith are not just colourful accounts of the ancient past; they provide purpose, meaning, and guidance for living in the present also. For example, Christians telling again the Christmas story of Jesus' birth in an outhouse to a migrant mother find themselves constrained to take the issue of homelessness seriously. Hindus celebrating the triumph of Ram and Sita's faithful love over the wiles of the evil Ravana are reminded of the central importance of safeguarding the family structures which lie at the heart of their culture. While individual believers will of course live out their lives in individually different ways, still in these and similar ways whole communities characteristically associate with themselves a broadly defined set of values, of ethical and philosophical principles to guide their lives. Within the faith of the community, these principles are then understood as being related to the ultimate structure of divine reality itself.

Such values expressed in the life of faith communities can be a powerful catalyst in the task of building up a sense of community in wider society also, particularly in some of the deprived inner areas of our cities. It is here that the most people of non-Christian faiths still live, alongside many Christians and many others with no specific faith commitment. These people of faith are a great resource in the lives of our cities, for their communities can motivate and mobilise local people in urban regeneration through inviting them to work out in practice the values and hopes their faith affords them.

Seeing communities being built up like this with the support of faith-based values, it is natural to ask, as many have, whether different faith groups cannot come together to build up a 'community of communities', both locally and nationally. It is important to understand what is being envisaged here. This is certainly not a question of an over-arching 'super-religion', nor even of the 'integration' of people of different faiths into a common religious culture. All are concerned that the distinctive integrity of each faith community should be preserved; indeed, just as the separate religious groups themselves encompass widely differing strands, so to a much greater extent any authentic community of communities must be built on a firm avowal of the principle of diversity. That means that we should not be trying to avoid disagreements and even controversies, but rather building inter-community links that are strong enough to recognise and handle such differences. People of faith in Britain today are in some places and contexts beginning to reach such a stage. One of the most notable instances is provided by the often heated but generally creative discussions that accompanied the formulation of new local school syllabi for religious education.

That educational process also illustrated the degree to which, alongside the disagreements, there is a considerable convergence in values between the great traditions of the world's faiths: for example, in areas such as respect for the dignity of the individual, a common quest for justice and peace, a concern to safeguard the integrity of the natural world, a value placed on honesty and stability in family and other relationships, a recognition of the importance of equipping young people to play a responsible role in society, and, above all, a stress on the need to limit material consumption since the ultimate goal of human life lies in a transcendent or spiritual end. Some of the most fruitful areas of inter-faith dialogue in Britain in the future may well centre around such shared values; it will be interesting to see whether such dialogue can move beyond the stage of reaching a consensus between people of faith, to become a basis on which they can together speak and act prophetically in society.

Such a convergence of values will be no surprise to those acquainted with the pattern of catholic ethical thought. The tradition of natural law theology, though it was sometimes applied in the past in a rather inflexible way, spoke of the existence of general principles of ethical guidance which were accessible to all who in good faith sought the good. Detailed courses of action were not understood to be prescribed directly by the natural law; the formation of actual plans in any given situation was dependent on a complex interplay of individual conscience, community consensus, and general ethical principles, all operating within the constraints of the given situation. It would be foolhardy to attempt a simple transposition into the multi-faith society of modern Britain of the categories of classical natural law thought. Nevertheless, there may yet be much to learn from the underlying methods and motivations of those ways of thinking which proved so congenial to faith in the past. Contemporary Christians who take seriously the challenge to build up together a community of communities must be in constant dialogue with our own traditions as well as with one another, and in that dialogue we will be defining together an area of shared values from which we can witness together to our neighbours.

Such a shared responsibility for building community derives in the last analysis from the fact that people of all faiths, including Christians, are living together under God in one and the same society. That implies a shared responsibility for the place where we live and for the way in which we relate to it – locally and globally.

Sharing a Common Home

'Praised be You, My Lord, with all your creatures, especially Sir Brother Sun, Who is the day and through whom You give us light. And he is beautiful and radiant with great splendour; and bears a likeness of You, Most High One'

St Francis of Assisi, *'Canticle of Brother Sun'*

In 1986, the Worldwide Fund for Nature invited leaders of different world faiths to Assisi to join with conservationists and ecologists in committing themselves to care of the environment on the basis of their respective beliefs and practices. The Hindus, Buddhists, Muslims, Christians and Jews present issued a series of 'Declarations on Nature', spelling out how each community understood its faith as shaping believers' relationships with the natural world. Since that time, the common concern of people of faith for our world has grown: Sikhs, Jains, and Bahais have also issued Declarations; networks of people of all faiths sharing ecological concerns have been established across the world; practically oriented schemes to preserve and enhance the environment have sprung up locally with religious support; educational programmes and theological explorations relating to environmental issues have developed apace in different faith communities.

This growing interaction between religion and ecology operates in two ways. On one hand, many who have been deeply involved in the environmental movement find that involvement leading them to search for a spiritual underpinning, a vision of the world that will give an overall context to their practical action. In this context we can place the diffuse movements of spirituality, philosophy and lifestyle which go under the name of 'New Age'. Certainly much of this is confused, ephemeral and religiously illiterate. However, there is also much of value, and the whole phenomenon points to serious issues which people of faith need to address; the deep concern with the passivity of mother earth as source and support of life in particular serves as something of a corrective to traditional western religious emphases on activity, transcendence, and patriarchy.

The second direction in which religious ecological concern manifests itself is through members of the established faith communities facing up to the magnitude of the ecological crisis confronting our world and realising the need to renew the insights and challenges which their faiths open up to them in relating to the environment.

Christians in particular are becoming aware of the extent to which their faith has been narrowed down in an anthropocentric direction. God's words to men and women in Genesis; 'Be fruitful and multiply, and fill the earth and subdue it; and have dominion over the fish of the sea and over the birds of the air and over every living thing that moves upon the earth' (Genesis 1.28) have been misinterpreted as a licence for reckless exploitation of natural resources and ill-treatment of other animals; the doctrine of creation has been largely eclipsed by that of the 'Fall'; the potential scope of salvation has generally been dogmatically restricted to the human species; little attention has been paid to the cosmic work of the Spirit, who 'breathed over the face of the waters' at the beginning (Genesis 1.2), in whom 'the whole creation groans together in travail' (Romans 8.22), who can be seen and experienced as 'a unifying force pulsating through the lives of all human beings – but not just the pulsating force in the lives of all human species, but the life giving force providing life for all the species in our spirit graced, spirit filled universe'.[7]

Yet the choice of Assisi for the 1986 gathering serves to remind us also of alternative strands in Christian history, including the Catholic tradition. The 'Canticle of Brother Sun', for example, came from one who

> could not walk upon stones without reverence and awe for love of Him who is the keystone of the corner ... he would not let them cut all the wood from a tree to light the fire, for love of Him who wrought our salvation on the wood of the Cross ... he lived continuously in the midst of a forest of symbols, and the living reality of this symbolism was so living that by it he regulated all his actions.[8]

The entire universe was for Francis sacramental of the glory and the love of the God he knew in Christ. In Catholic understanding, the sacramental status of the earth reaches its fullest expression in the sacrifice of the mass, when the natural substances of wheat and grapes, transformed first by human work into bread and wine, are then further infused by divine grace to become the bearers of life and salvation. Not only is there here an affirmation of the value of the created order in God's eyes; there is also the recognition of the special responsibility of stewardship and renewal which humans have as priests in that order.

In recovering a living sense of our place within God's creation, Christians can learn much from other faith traditions – for example, from the Jain vision of the cosmos as home to a vast number of living beings, all of whom are linked together by bonds of interdependence and mutual support. Jains aim to cause no harm or injury to any living being – so, for example, Jain monks and nuns will carefully sweep the ground before they tread on it, lest they should inadvertently squash small insects; Jainism enjoins a strictly vegetarian diet. Much in this would be inappropriate in a different cultural setting, but the underlying vision of the whole world as sacred can be shared by people of all faiths, including Christians.

Here we see living proof of what has justifiably been called a wider 'ecumenism'. The word in common usage has come to mean 'interdenominational', but its true import cannot be limited to the Christian family. Like 'ecology', it derives from the Greek root 'oikos', a 'home': the 'oikoumene' is the whole inhabited world – that is to say, ecumenism brings together all who live in the one common home, the complex and interlocking eco-system which is our planet. To get our ecology right is a vital concern for all of us who share that one common home, and it is a concern in which the faiths by which we live will play a formative role. Moreover, this concern is not just a luxury for the affluent: ecological concern for the integrity of creation must always operate in tandem with economic concern for a more just society.

People of faith become involved in these eco-concerns at every level. Indeed, they are involved already, whether they realise it or not; those who are not providing part of the answer are providing part of the problem through uncritically participating in systems of wasteful consumption, unjust distribution, and environmental destruction.

While global summits and policy consultations play a vital role in co-ordinating action, the answers of faith often speak with a particular cogency at the level of local communities and individual lifestyles. A church, mosque or temple establishes a recycling scheme on its premises; a group of people of faith work together to enhance their local environment; an individual believer walks or cycles more and drives less, reducing consumption and sending the balance saved to a development scheme in the two-thirds world. These are small steps, yet they spring from elements deeply embedded in faith. Thus they have a special value as lived parables of the faithful's commitment to respect and renew the world which they share as a common home.

One symbol perhaps has a special resonance today as a sign both of that commitment and of the corresponding hope of its fulfilment which faith expresses: the symbol of the tree. In traditional Hindu cosmology, the world-tree holds together the various levels of the cosmos; a similar myth of Yggdrasill, the tree which linked the worlds of gods and men and guarded their life, was known to the Norse and Teutonic forbears of the English. The Buddha achieved his enlightenment sitting under a **bodhi** tree, and Christian tradition speaks of the cross of the risen Christ as the 'tree of life.' Further, the Bible's final vision of the heavenly city has at its centre, this same tree, its leaves for the healing of the nations (Revelation 22.2).

That vision, with its picture of humane urban society reintegrated into harmony within the cosmic order, is surely an appropriate one for an age in which the most dramatic sign of our environmental alienation is the horrifying destruction of tropical rainforests. All people of faith can share here a common mission of recalling the oikoumene to ecological responsibility; that mission will be nurtured by the rediscovery of ecumenical archetypical symbols like that of the life-giving tree.

Proclaiming Good News

'Quite the opposite of propaganda is evangelization, filled with hope, which means moving forward in a world with unlimited possibilities, in which we won't be surprised if something unforeseen happens'

Vincent Donovan, *'Christianity Rediscovered – An Epistle from the Masai'*

At the beginning of Jesus' ministry, the first three gospels agree that he came into Galilee 'proclaiming the good news of God' (Mark 1.14, cf Luke 4.14, Matthew 4.17), and evangelism, the proclamation of God's good news, has always been a primary impulse for Christians. In this respect, Christianity differs radically from some other faiths, which do not stress such a missionary element. On the other hand, it has much in common with others for example Islam, where **da'wah** has been defined as:

> the fulfilment of the commandment 'to call men unto the path of Allah'. Besides, it is the efforts by the Muslim to enable other men to share and benefit from the supreme vision, the religious truth, which he has appropriated. In this respect it is rationally necessary, for truth wants to be known. It exerts pressure on the knower to share his vision of it with his peers.[9]

That definition identifies two motivations for **da'wah**: first, an express scriptural injunction, understood to be the divine will ('the fulfilment of the commandment'), and second, the inherent logic of the message itself, which demands its wider telling ('rationally necessary'). In asking how Christians can proclaim good news sensibly and sensitively in a multi-faith society, it may therefore be helpful to bear in mind these two questions. First, what do the gospels themselves show as a pattern of evangelism? And secondly, where are we led by the inner logic of telling the story of our faith?

The first thing to notice in the gospels is the difference between evangelism and discipling. Jesus first proclaims the good news to the village communities of Galilee; then he singles out certain individuals, the fishermen, to follow him (Matthew 4, Mark 1, Luke 4). In the 'Great Commission' (Matthew 28.19), those to be evangelised are not individuals but nations.

The second thing the gospels show is that words are by no means the only media Jesus uses in his proclamation of the good news. The inbreaking of the kingdom is communicated by acts of healing and deliverance, by miraculous signs and wonders, by the celebration of great feasts of fellowship and reconciliation. Perhaps the most characteristic mark of the good news is the way in which it establishes new relationships of forgiveness and friendship where previously there had been grievance and alienation – relationships which encompass God and humans, 'sinners' and 'righteous', men and women, Jew and Gentile (Luke 23.12), and which cluster around the reconciling figure of Jesus himself. Where Jesus does use words it is in the context of story-telling, which meets people where they are, takes up the themes of their own situation and discloses to them the boundless grace of God's kingdom which is bursting into the lives they are already living.

So if evangelism is to be patterned on the gospels we must, first, remember that our task is the proclamation of good news, not the making of new Christians. The freedom and confidence which the Spirit mediates are surely impaired by attempts to force people to respond by abandoning one way of faith for another; indeed, such attempts sometimes seem to betray a deep-seated lack of confidence in faith and a narrow understanding of the gospel which does not do justice to Paul's insight that 'for freedom Christ has set us free' (Galatians 5.1). We must also find ways of relating the good news to the collective concerns and aspirations of other faith communities, rather than picking off individual members.

In addressing that good news, words will form only one aspect of our witness. The demonstration of a genuine concern for healing and liberation, evidence of a real openness to the wonderful grace of God at work in his world, the forging of new relationships of partnership and friendship in place of mistrust and enmity – it is by these things that the good news is most powerfully proclaimed. People of non-Christian faith will often view with considerable suspicion the overtures of Christians eager to share the gospel with them; misguided and mishandled proselytising enthusiasm can still cause untold damage to relations between Christians and other people of faith, perhaps especially between Christians and Jews, where the shadow of the past is in any case particularly dark. Only by a genuine willingness to be alongside the other in humility, and sometimes in silence, can our credibility be restored.

Once real relationships have been established, Christians may find that there are times when faith is naturally shared in words. Like Jesus, we will most often end up doing this by telling stories – stories of our individual lives that have been crossed by the grace of God in Christ, stories of our communities which embody the good news in their collective lives, stories of Jesus and the saints in whom we have seen light, and stories which are not religious in a conventional sense, yet which speak of transcendent hope and meaning. These stories must have grasped us and become part of the fabric of our lives; if they have not, then they are not our own faith, and we would do better to keep silence.

We cannot be tellers of stories unless we are hearers also: we must be ready to listen to the stories of faith which our friends will want to share with us. However different may be the presuppositions from which these stories begin and the conclusion to which they point, we will often find that something along the way will speak to the heart of our own life. When a new dimension is opened up in our own vision, or a forgotten aspect of our own faith is renewed, we ourselves are evangelised.

That sense in which stories from one faith tradition can evoke a deep resonance in people of another tradition should cause us to be wary of any attempt to identify **the distinctive** content of evangelism as being some element of Christian faith which by definition non-Christians cannot accept (for example, the doctrine of the atoning death of Christ) and then to rank all other aspects of Christian proclamation as secondary matters. If we do that, we may end up saying things like this:

> We wholeheartedly support co-operation in appropriate community, social, moral and political issues between Christians and those of other faiths wherever this is possible. Nevertheless, we believe it to be our Lord's command that his Gospel be clearly proclaimed, openly and sensitively, to all people (including those of other faiths) with the intention that they should come to faith in him for salvation.[10]

That word 'nevertheless' reflects a circumscribed view of the gospel, and so of evangelism: the gospel is understood to be precisely that which distinguishes Christians, who have access to this good news, from others, who by definition do not. If the gospel is what it must be – good news from God – then it is to be affirmed wherever it may be found. In witnessing to the divine life and truth which has grasped me in Jesus, as I must, I need not be denigrating the witness of my brother or sister that divine life and truth has grasped him or her in some other way.

The limits on God's self-communication which we constantly seek to impose derive largely from our fear that we will lose our identity if we do not define ourselves as being opposed to others. But in the central mystery of Christian faith we encounter a trinity of persons who receive and express their identity, not in opposition to, but in complementary relationship with, one another. More affirmative and open patterns of evangelism could build on that understanding of divine identity to show that our Christian identity need not be defined as being what separates us from other communities of faith; more positively, it could be that which enables us in confidence and freedom to enter into creative relationship with others.

It is of course in the figure of Jesus Christ that Christians will find the primary positive focus of their community identity. Within such a context of relationship, an important question for the Christian community will be, how it is to understand that focal figure whom we confess as Lord.

Confessing Jesus as Lord

'In the wonder of the incarnation your eternal Word has brought to the eyes of faith a new and radiant vision of your glory. In him we see our God made visible and so are caught up in love of the God we cannot see'

Roman Missal, Preface of the Incarnation

'Jesus Christ is Lord' – this is one of the basic statements of Christian faith from the time of the New Testament onwards, and christological thought ever since has been concerned to find a satisfactory way in which this confession of faith can be expressed in terms accessible to contemporary understanding.

Writing to the church at Corinth, St Paul balanced the basic credal statement by another, which related it to the context of himself and of the people he was addressing: 'what we preach is not ourselves, but Jesus Christ as Lord, with ourselves as your servants for Jesus' sake' (2 Corinthians 4.5). Paul was concerned that the proclamation of the lordship of Jesus should not be heard as an exaltation of the apostolic office; more than this, throughout these chapters of 2 Corinthians he paradoxically couples his vision of the glorified Jesus with an account of Christians as being broken, abased, 'given up to death' (2 Corinthians 4.11).

These may not be phrases that spring naturally to our minds in speaking of the situation of Christians in contemporary Britain. Nevertheless, the fundamental tension Paul experienced belongs to us also: we need to find ways of expressing our faith in the triumph of Jesus as Lord without being triumphalistic. And we need to remember that 'triumphalism' is a contextual term. Simply to avow an intention of confessing our faith in humility and brokenness is not enough; we need also to listen to how our confession is in fact heard by those outside our faith. We can develop this point by recalling the distinction drawn by Jesus himself between the appropriation of truth by Christian disciples and its reception by the wider world when he tells the twelve: 'To you has been given the secret of the kingdom of God, but for those outside everything is in parables (Mark 4.11). Catholic Christianity in its first few centuries was to evolve the so-called **disciplina arcani**, the deliberate restriction of full access to Christian sacramental life and truth to those fully initiated as disciples.

It is against this background that we are to set orthodox formulations such as the Council of Chalcedon's definition in 451 of the union of perfect divinity and perfect humanity in the person of Jesus. This must be seen as the result of a long, internal dynamic within the Christian community to understand the significance of Jesus' lordship; it cannot be wrenched from that community context as a prepackaged propositional truth with which to confront people of other faith traditions.

But this does not mean a complete divorce between the Christian confession of Jesus as Lord and the ways in which people of other faiths view him. On one hand, there are strands within the Christian tradition that provide an account of Jesus' significance which makes space for openness to people of other faiths; on the other, many people outside the Christian tradition see in Jesus' life and ministry a deeply significant pattern of divine involvement in the world.

Probably the most influential Christian attempt to explain the significance of Jesus in inclusive terms has arisen from the application of the expression 'logos', 'word', to Christ in the Johannine writings. Understanding the logos to be the creative, supportive, integrative principle of rationality and order, rooted in the divine life, which gives meaning and purpose to the world, and which is especially congruent to humanity, one influential school of Christian thought has developed John's teaching that 'the true light that enlightens every person was coming into the world' (John 1.9), into an acknowledgement of the presence of that same 'logos' in other traditions of human faith and thought. In the second-century apologists such as Justin Martyr, for example, this served as an explanation of the perceived holiness and goodness of pre-Christian philosophers like Plato and Socrates: 'each [of the philosophers, the poets, and others], through his share in the divine generative Logos, spoke well, seeing what was akin to it ... for all those writers were able, through the seed of the Logos implanted in them, to see reality darkly'.[11]

Again, in our own century William Temple broadened the scope of the 'logos' doctrine, in words that have become famous, to include other, living faiths:

> All that is noble in the non-Christian systems of thought, or conduct, or worship is the work of Christ upon them and within them. By the Word of God – that is to say, by Jesus Christ – Isaiah, and Plato, and Zoroaster, and Buddha, and Confucius conceived and uttered such truths as they declared. There is only one divine light; and every man in his measure is enlightened by it.[12]

Temple's words may now seem rather dated. For one thing, we must surely admit that 'the work of Christ' is only 'all that is noble in Christianity' as much as in the 'non-Christian systems': Christianity as much as other religions is a complex amalgam of the divine and the demonic, the life-giving and the death-dealing. Also, the somewhat stilted references to the conception and utterance of truth by a galaxy of worthies including 'Plato, Zoroaster, Buddha, and Confucius' hardly provide an adequate frame of reference for dealing with the faiths of hundreds of millions of people alive today.

However, to accuse Temple's logos-based inclusivism of being a thinly veiled form of Christian colonialism, as is often done, is surely unrealistic, for it is difficult to see how we can understand differing faith systems other than in terms drawn ultimately from our own. Our formative perception of ultimate reality is that God is as he is in Christ. Accordingly, our ultimate criterion in assessing divine involvement in reality must be that of 'Christlikeness' – 'does this agree with God as we know him in Jesus?' This seems to me to be the heart of the logos-doctrine, as of related motifs like F.D. Maurice's insistence that Christ is the 'head of every man' or the biblical allusions to Christ as the 'wisdom' (**sophia**) of God. These all provide promising avenues of approach to other faiths, providing they are coupled with awareness of other formative perceptions of ultimate reality and with a willingness to engage in dialogue with them.

Space for that awareness and motivation for that dialogue are perhaps provided by the Trinitarian context of orthodox Christology. For the incarnation displays a distinctive pattern in which Jesus relates as Son to God as Father. It is by no means obvious that such a pattern could not be complemented by other patterns of relationship between the world and God. Christology, exploring the significance of the Father-Son relationship, would not then necessarily be 'in competition' with other traditions of reflection on other patterns of divine encounter with created being. Belief in the Trinity affirms the constitutive role of the Spirit in the relationship with the Father which gives Jesus his deepest identity – it is at the baptismal descent of the Spirit that the Father's voice declares, 'You are my beloved Son' (Mark 1.11).

Yet the dispensation of the Spirit cannot be pinned down to christological formulae, since freedom and diversity are of its very nature. It is, for example, within the realm of the Spirit's 'leading into all truth' that we should locate the responses that many people of non-Christian faith make to the event of Jesus Christ. The story of Gandhi's fascination with the figure of Jesus is well known. He loved to sing the hymn 'When I survey the wondrous cross', and on the wall of his ashram hung a picture of Christ with the words 'In him is our peace'. What was said of him could be said of many people of non-Christian faith before and since: 'he had a very special sense of kinship with the Son of Man who collected dust on his feet on the rocky path to Mount Olivet, who went about doing good and who fell foul of the authorities, including the leaders of his own community'.[13]

No account of Jesus' significance can claim to be truly 'catholic', in the sense of whole and complete, if it does not value the immense appeal that he has had for countless people of other faiths. Many such people find in the life and teaching of Jesus a powerful disclosure of divine truth and grace, yet strongly repudiate any attempt by the Christian church to 'own' the figure of one who rightly belongs to humanity and all its communities. For example, Jesus is held in very special regard as a prophet by the Muslim community – the Quran, while apparently rejecting the gospel accounts of his crucifixion, affirms his virgin birth, miraculous deeds, and divine vocation to prophethood – and modern Jews are rediscovering the charismatic Jewish teacher from Galilee. These interpretations of the Christ story reflect the faith to which they belong; the result is a kaleidoscope of images which Christians can find both exhilarating and somewhat disorientating.

Where does all this leave us? It leaves us, I believe, with a double agenda: first, to affirm our Christian faith in Jesus as Lord in ways which are free of triumphalism at every level, and second, to relate our own affirmations to the images of Jesus reflected in other faith communities. We can begin to see this process happening in the later books of the New Testament canon, as the language and thought forms of the Gentile world take their place alongside Jewish categories in the attempt to reflect fully the experience of the one who had 'broken down the dividing wall of hostility . . . that he migh create in himself one new man' (Ephesians 2.14f). That ministry of reconciliation is in catholic understanding particularly associated with the priestly office of Jesus, and in Latin tradition a high-priest is a **pontifex**, a 'builder of bridges'. So we in our multi-faith generation must seek to find images of Jesus' significance that build bridges across the barriers which divide our shared humanity.

It is certainly too soon to say what the eventual shape of the christological picture will be, but some themes may be apparent already. Christians will always look to Jesus as the primary icon in whom we see the divine relating to the world. The reality signified by the icon is a loving bond of Father and Son, which is yet, in the power of the Spirit, inviting to all. Other icons of the absolute in relation to the contingent may highlight different aspects of reality, but a growing humility will point us to a proper reserve in asserting the primacy of one over another for all people.

Perhaps one of the most helpful symbols, accessible to people of every faith, will be that of light. It is this image which St Paul uses writing to the Corinthians: 'the God who said 'Out of darkness let light shine!' is the same God who made his light shine in our hearts, to bring us the light of the knowledge of God's glory, shining in the face of Christ' (2 Corinthians 4.6). The same God, because he is the creator and father of all people, has never left himself without witnesses to that glory, and his light is seen by others shining in the face of the Lord Krishna, the Buddha, the Prophet, holy figures of all faiths. Commenting on Paul's words, St Ambrose relates them to the dramatic change wrought in the life of Zacchaeus by his encounter with Christ: 'He saw Christ and he found light, he saw him and he who had been robbing others of their goods now was happy to give away his own!'[14] People of other faiths too can say that they have 'found light'; and that encounter, mediated by whatever icon of the divine, has set them, like Zacchaeus, on a path of self-overcoming which leads them further into the life of God.

Travelling to the Father

'I want to seek out a means of going to heaven by a little way, a way that is very straight, very short, and totally new'

St Thérèse of Lisieux, '*Histoire d' Une Ame*'

One of the scriptural texts most frequently quoted by those wishing to discount the possibility of any saving significance in other ways of faith is the reply of Jesus to Thomas at the Last Supper 'I am the way, and the truth, and the life; no one comes to the Father, but by me (John 14.6). These words, of course, cannot be detached from the context in which John sets them – namely, a journey which reaches through death and life to the Father. Jesus himself is to make this journey, and he teaches the disciples that they must join him on it. As so often in John's gospel, they only partly understand what he says:

> [JESUS] ... you know the way where I am going.
> [THOMAS] Lord, we do not know where you are going; how can we know the way?
> [JESUS] I am the way ... If you had known me, you would have known my Father also; henceforth you know him and have seen him.
> [PHILIP] Lord, show us the Father, and we shall be satisfied.
> [JESUS] Have I been with you so long, and yet you do not know me, Philip? He who has seen me has seen the Father ... (John 14.3–9).

Jesus is here redefining the basic concept of 'way'. Philip and Thomas both understand a way to be simply a means of getting from A to B, and they consequently share a preoccupation with the goal to which the way leads. In Jesus' teaching, however, the way is not simply a means of reaching the Father. It is the way itself, himself, that is presented to the disciples, to which, to whom, they must respond, on which, supported by whom, they must walk. It is in that walking that the disciple is to realise an intense communion, both with the goal and with the way himself – a communion grounded in the unity that exists between the way and the goal, the Son and the Father. And so Jesus will go on (John 14.15ff, 25ff) to make to the disciples the promise of the Paraclete, the Holy Spirit, that assurance of support and guidance with them on the pilgrim way which has been described as the presence of Jesus when he is absent.

As the Christ presents this challenge to his disciples, so the way confronts us and invites us to walk upon it. As Catholic faith teaches that God the Son is coequal and consubstantial with God the Father, so the way cannot be subordinated to or divorced from the goal to which it leads. As the Spirit leads the disciples into the heart of the divine relationship of love, so in treading the way we are conscious of oneness with the goal: 'Christianity is not an ideology, philosophy, or theology, or a set of ideas about God: Christianity is not anything, it is somebody: Jesus and the resurrection'.[15]

The theme of 'way' or 'path' is in fact central in the world's great faith traditions:

> Religions are not first and foremost institutionalised systems but Ways. Aren't the Old and New Testaments full of talk about the Way of the Lord? Weren't the first Christians called followers of the Way (Acts 9.2)? Doesn't the first Sura of the Koran talk about the straight Way? Doesn't Hinduism know three Ways to salvation? Doesn't Buddhism talk about the Eightfold Path?[16]

And there is in the understanding of 'way' a stress on the here-and-now imperative to walk on the path which presents itself, without clinging either to the achievement of having covered some distance already or to the assurance of a detailed knowledge of what the goal will be.

For example, it is well-known that the last of the 'Four Noble Truths' enunciated by the Buddha is that of the **magga** – the teaching that the 'noble eightfold path' is the sure route to enlightenment. Early Buddhism interpreted this as meaning: to get from your present benighted condition to the condition of enlightenment, you must follow this path, for the way serves just as a route to reach the goal. In subsequent developments of the tradition, however, 'the way' itself becomes the priority. Indeed, 'seeking after enlightenment' can become a false aspiration as the seeker wrongfully clings to this goal. One must simply practise the way of disciplined meditation without concern for the future: 'To study the Way is to try to become one with it – to forget even a trace of enlightenment. Those who would practise the Way should first of all believe in it. Those who believe in the Way should believe they have been in the Way from the beginning'.[17]

Likewise, the people of Israel were constantly to recall their pilgrim roots – 'A wandering Aramean was my father' (Deuteronomy 26.5) – and the early Christians too understood themselves to be those who 'have here no lasting city, but seek the city which is to come' (Hebrews 13.14). Nor is this a vision shared only by Jews, Christians and Buddhists; people of other faiths also interpret the spiritual life as travelling on a journey, walking a way.

Of course, we cannot know for certain that they are travelling on the same way as we are, but it is possible to interpret John 14.6 thus. Jesus' words to Thomas, as they invite us to travel with him on the way, name that way as himself. If a way to 'come to the Father' does in fact enter into the lives of men and women of other faiths, then we are encouraged to say that what our brothers and sisters are experiencing is an invitation to travel on this same way which we know as Christ, for apart from that way indeed nobody can come to the Father.

The plausibility of such a claim is enhanced by the setting of the Lord's words, on the night before he died, for this points us to the essential character of the way. It is a constant dying to self, in that we leave behind old, false images of who we are, and their projections as equally false images of who God is, to travel ceaselessly into the boundless reality of the true God who, giving himself in constant selflessness, invites us to do the same. The themes of resolute self-overcoming, of an arduous quest for deeper truth, and of entry into a world of ineffable mystery, are again marks found in faith traditions throughout the world, so much so that we may even be justified in speaking of a common pilgrimage into God.

It is in such a context that dialogue may acquire its deepest expression through the occasional possibility of shared prayer, meditation, worship, silence. These things have generally been discussed in the context of religious communities expressing their own identities, not compromising their integrity, while coming together in fellowship. There are certainly times when this is an important issue, but there are other contexts for shared worship – times when the identity of worshippers is not to be proclaimed in distinction from others, but rather to find its true fulfilment through self-forgetfulness in the presence of the transcendent wonder of the God who infinitely exceeds all our limited preconceptions of him. Worship of this type will move out from a reliance on verbal expression, cerebral acceptance and confessional response, to incorporate shared silence, common symbols like water or light, and space for each person to be open to the numinous in their own terms. In this, it will of course be congruent with traditional Catholic patterns of liturgy which have always given liberty to individuals to pursue their own devotional paths within the corporate context of worship.

The pursuit of the pilgrimage of faith is not to be understood in any faith as an escape from the real world. On the contrary, it is an entering more deeply into the reality of the created order as we enter more deeply into the reality of the Creator. Jesus' words link 'the way' with 'the truth' and 'the life', and in this Christians and people of other faiths share the experience that their commitment to the religious quest both leads them into new truth – fresh perspectives on themselves, their families and friends, their societies and their world – and gives them access to new life – hope in the face of death, injustice and decay, love and patience to conquer hatred and distrust, the forging of new relationships and the creation of a new spirit.

These are things which Christians know in their own lives, and they are things which are readily discernible in the lives of our brothers and sisters of other faiths also. As we travel along the way whom we know to be Christ, we know that they too are treading ways where truth and life abound. None of us at any time has seen the goal of any of those ways, but may we not suppose that they too are travelling to the one God and Father of us all?

References

1. Pope Gregory VII, Letter to the Muslim ruler of Bijaya (1076), quoted in Nadir Dinshaw, *A Wide-Open Heart: An interfaith anthology of Christian comment* (Christian Action, 1992), p3

2. Michael Barnes, 'Faith meets Faith', *The Month*, Sep/Oct 1991

3. William Blake, 'The Fly', *Songs of Experience*, 1794

4. William Shakespeare, *The Merchant of Venice*, Act iii, scene 1

5. Martin Forward, ed, *God of all Faith* (Methodist Church Home Mission Division, 1989), pp20f

6. Thomas Butler, *Still Faith in the City?* (Leeds University Lecture, 1992)

7. Ivor Smith-Cameron, 'Paradigm Shifts in Global Christianity', in *Ambassador* No 2 (Church of England General Synod Board of Mission, 1991), p7

8. Etienne Gilson, *The Philosophy of St Bonaventure* (St Anthony Guild, 1965), p65

9. Isma'il al-Faruqi, 'On the Nature of Islamic Da'wah', p33, in *Christian Mission and Islamic Da'wah – Proceedings of the Chambesy Dialogue Consultation* [1976] (Islamic Foundation, 1982)

10. 'An Open Letter to the Leadership of the Church of England' [on 'multi-faith worship'] *Church Times*, Dec 1991

11. Justin Martyr, 'Apologia II', xiii, in Henry Bettenson (ed), *The Early Christian Fathers: A Selection from the Writings of the Fathers from St Clement of Rome to St Athanasius* (Oxford, 1976), pp63f

12. William Temple, *Readings in St John's Gospel* (Macmillan, 1961), p9, quoted in Kenneth Cracknell, *Towards A New Relationship: Christians and People of Other Faiths* (Epworth, 1986), p103

13. Margaret Chatterjee, *Gandhi's Religious Thought* (Macmillan, 1983), p56

14. St Ambrose of Milan, 'Discourses on the Psalms', 43.90, from *The Divine Office* (Collins, 1974), vol iii, p341

15. Michael Marshall, *The Gospel Connection: A Study in Evangelism for the Nineties* (Darton, Longman & Todd, 1991)

16. Arnulf Camps, *Partners in Dialogue* (Orbis, 1983), p84, quoted in Kenneth Cracknell, op cit, pp78f

17. Dogen, 'Gakudo Yojin-shu' ('Points to Watch in Buddhist Training' [1234]), ix, p57, in Yuho Yokoi, *Zen Master Dogen* (Weatherhill, 1976)